How to
MASTER
the PRINCIPLES of
Wealth

Discover the secrets of the wealthy and find out how common people are creating uncommon income.

DR. MIKEL BROWN

How to Master the Principles of Wealth

CJC PUBLISHING COMPANY

1208 S Sumac Dr
El Paso, TX 79925

Copyright © 2006 by Mikel Brown. All rights reserved
Printed in the United States of America

ISBN:978-1-930388-16-1

Editorial assistance for CJC Publishing Co. by Gary Sparkman
Cover design by CJC Publishing Co.

All quotations is appropriately noted after the quote

No part of this publication may be reproduced, stored in a retrieval system, or transmitted in any form or by any means, electronic, mechanical, photocopying, recording, scanning, or otherwise, except as permitted under Section 107 or 108 of the 1976 United States Copyright Act, without the prior written permission of the Published. Requests to the Publisher for permission should be addreded to the Permissions Department, CJC Publishing, 1208 Sumac Drive. El Paso, TX 79925, 915-595-137, fax 915-595-1493, or e-mail permcoordinator@cjcpublishing.com.

Limit of Liability/Disclaimer of Warranty: While the publisher and author have used their best efforts in preparing this book, they make no representation or warranties with respect to the accuracy or completeness of the contents of this book and specifically disclaim any implied guarantees. The advice and strategies contained herein may not be suitable for every situation. Neither the publisher nor author shall be liable for any outcome concerning ones finances or business, included but not limited to special, incidental, consequential, or other damages.

Table of Content

The Easy Way To Master Wealth 5

Eight Things Wealthy People Do 11

Mastering The Fundamentals Of Success 25

Secrets To Personal Success 29

Money Tips 35

It's Good To Be A Winner 43

First Principles of Wealth The Groundwork of Increase 47

The Easy Way To Master Wealth

"The rich see opportunities to work and invest their money, and in their ideas."

~ **Mikel Brown**

The Easy Way To Master Wealth

BUILDING WEALTH IS A JOURNEY that begins with understanding fundamental principles and applying them consistently. It's not just for the elite or the lucky few; it's an achievable goal for everyone, including young individuals. The beauty of wealth building is that age is not a barrier; even a twelve-year-old can embark on this enriching journey.

Start Small, Dream Big

Imagine you're building a magnificent castle, but instead of stones, your building blocks are your savings and investments. Just as every castle starts with a single stone, your wealth begins with your first saved dollar. The key is to start small. Even if it's just a few dollars from your allowance or a birthday gift, saving a portion is the first step towards building wealth.

The Magic of Compound Interest

Albert Einstein famously called compound interest the eighth wonder of the world. Why? Because it allows your money to grow exponentially over time. If you save $100 and it grows at 5% per year, in the next year, you'll not only earn interest on your original $100 but also on the interest it has already earned. Over years and decades, this growth can be astonishing. It's like planting a tree; at first, it grows slowly, but over time, it becomes a towering giant.

Budgeting: Your Financial Compass

Budgeting is like having a map on your wealth-building journey. It helps you understand where your money is going and ensures you're not spending more than you earn. A simple way to budget, is the 50-30-20 rule: spend 50% on needs, 30% on wants, and invest and save 20%. This method helps in distinguishing between essentials and luxuries.

Investing: Not Just for Adults

Investing might sound complex, but it's just a way to make your money work for you. You don't have to be a stock market expert; start with something simple. For instance, if you're passionate about video games or a particular brand, consider investing a small amount in their stocks. This way, you're not just a consumer but a part-owner of the company.

Education: The Best Investment

Investing in your education and skills is the most valuable investment. Learning about money management, reading books, or even attending workshops can equip you with knowledge that pays off for a lifetime. The more you learn, the better decisions you'll make about saving, spending, and investing. There is a one stop shop that can help in both the education process and the investment process by going online to www.ibelieveinvestment.com, tell them I sent you.

Patience and Consistency: The Secret Ingredients

Wealth building is not a sprint; it's a marathon. It requires patience and consistency. Just like how a tree doesn't bear fruit overnight, wealth doesn't grow immediately. It's about making small, smart choices regularly over a long period.

Embracing Failures as Lessons

Remember, it's okay to make mistakes. Every successful person has faced setbacks. The key is to learn from these experiences. Each failure is a step towards your goal, teaching you what doesn't work and bringing you closer to what does.

Conclusion: You're Never Too Young to Start

You're never too young to start building wealth. By mastering these principles, you're not just saving money; you're building a foundation for your future. It's about being smart with your money, no matter how small the amount. So, take that first step, no matter how small it seems. Remember, the journey of a thousand miles begins with a single step.

Eight Things Wealthy People Do

That Average People Won't Do

"The rich see opportunities to work and invest their money, and in their ideas."

~ **Mikel Brown**

Eight Things Wealthy People Do

That Average People Won't Do

THOSE WITH ENORMOUS WEALTH can influence the environment around them, and they have not failed in their attempts to do so. Those without wealth have to simply adapt to their environment. In the last 25 years, the share of total wealth held by the top 5 percent of the population has risen from sixteen to over twenty one percent. That top five percent now owns as much market wealth as the bottom sixty percent. Why does there exist such a disparity between the haves and the have-nots? High school diploma recipients have more than doubled and the number of college graduates has risen by a fraction of almost 4 times over the past twenty years. As education levels rise in this country, one would assume that income levels would rise as well. But this has not been the case. What can account for this discrepancy? Our universities are not teaching students to become entrepreneurs. Rather, they are instilling in students the desire to become high-paid indentured servants. People do not normally become very rich by placing their money in a savings account that only yields one percent or less. The rich seize opportunities to work and invest their money, and in their ideas.

The only reason some people are not wealthy is that they are unwilling to endure the struggles to qualify for the prize of success. People are people; good, bad, or indifferent. No individual owns the market on talent and ability. We all possess certain innate gifts that enable us to do some things better than others. None of us are born predisposed to be wealthy or poor. But there are many people who love to justify their station in life, by choosing to believe that they were born without the advantages that others seem to have. They settle for being neither rich nor poor, but average. Average individuals love to play it safe. They will shoot an arrow at a tree and then draw a target around it.

They live without goals for fear that they may not accomplish them. As I point out the eight things that wealthy people do, ask yourself this question; "Am I willing to do those things and take a risk?"

1. Wealthy people refuse to work for others.

Working for someone else is out of the question for these self-motivated people. They enjoy the liberty of being able to work without the hassle of someone watching over their shoulders. They have never truly been comfortable working for someone because their initiative and self-determination causes them to be at constant loggerheads with their bosses. Insecure managers usually prevent such self-driven individuals from coming into contact with company owners, for fear that the owners might recognize certain qualities in those individuals, and consequently, promote him or her. The unwillingness in some to work for anyone should not be construed as egotism. On the contrary, they are simply individuals with vision and goals of their own. They are those whose own futures cannot be neglected because of time-wasting attachments to the dreams of others.

2. Wealthy people work best under stress.

Stress for average people causes them to fall apart, whereas, the wealthy use the pressures of life to bring out their best. These purpose-driven individuals view eight hours of sleep as an unnecessary interruption from the pursuit of their dreams. A poll taken of the dominant characteristics of the wealthy reveals that these highly motivated people sleep an average of four hours a night. Not much sleep when you think about it! There are times when, because of the number of ideas racing in my mind, I simply cannot sleep. At times like these, it helps to be disciplined enough to jot down those ideas down, because the odds of losing them to memory are too great. You will be surprised by the wealth of ideas that come to you late at night. Remember! What you don't lose, you can use!

Wealthy people are seemingly inured to the pressures of life that slow the progress of ordinary individuals. To them, pressure is a normal part of life. They view pressure as a time for change from lesser to greater, smaller to bigger. Pressure does not make the man; it only exposes him for what he already is. You will never go far if you base your life on good intentions. Learn how to deal with the pressures of life, and you will be able to deal in business.

3. Wealthy people are usually motivated by their own imaginations and dreams.

Those who have labored to amass great wealth are usually quite astute in business, as well as, in life. Their ability to move forward, despite opposition, lies in the fact that they are guided by a clear and powerful vision. The ability to see into the future towards one's dream is a quality that forces self-made billionaires to forge ahead when everything around them is screaming to quit. The ability to dream, and the great pictures formed by wild imaginations are all the evidence they need to stay the course to achieve their objectives. Most people give up on the promise of their tomorrow because they have no photograph of the future that frames their hope. Successful businesspeople do not easily give up on their dreams, especially since the pictures they carry within of their successes are too precious to simply discard.

4. Wealthy people are willing to make opportunities where there aren't any.

If you truly want to know why these people are where they are financially... they are simply willing to do everything you are unwilling to do. There is a difference between looking for an opportunity and making one. Where there is no door to go through, successful people will stop looking for one so they can create a door. You cannot survive in business in a capitalist society by being passive and afraid to confront challenges. Success does not happen by accident, and neither is wealth created out of thin air. The problem with most people is that they would rather wait for someone else to give them a break. Wake up! You are that rich person with all the potential to build wealth. You must become a pioneer and lead the way for others to follow.

5. Wealthy people do not see quitting as an option.

Many people take great comfort in being able to simply throw in the towel and give up on their dreams when times are tough. Our ancestors understood well that as individuals thrive, so thrives the nation. This country did not prosper without the sacrifice of many. Wars tried this nation's right to exist, and the countless investments of inventions and ideas, that have all served to make America the most powerful and prosperous nation the world has ever known. Wars were fought to preserve our right to enjoy the spoils of capitalism, and to secure our nation's freedom. With similar fortitude have countless men and women been able to defy uncharted territories, to seize their wealth and prosperity. They realized the price that had to be paid, but found the courage to persevere knowing that others would benefit from their tenacity. Only those who possess the courage to fight through the lean and tough times are able to enjoy the fruit of wealth and prosperity.

6. Wealthy people are willing to be disliked and criticized.

There are many people who would like to enter your world for no other purpose than to stop you from succeeding. There is no reason why you should allow people to cast a shadow over your ability to make money. Unfortunately, we sometimes do. Friends, family members, and associates can all qualify as invalidators. Invalidators are people who operate in our lives, for no other purpose than to hinder us from achieving our success. Invalidators are the first to point out why your ideas will never work. Most of us can detect when people are trying to derail us from the path to our goals. But we may not be so quick to oppose the counterproductive efforts of invalidators, when our friends and family members are the perpetrators of such evil plots. They will give you 50 reasons why you are not qualified for a particular job, while all the while maintaining their friendship with you. You may be their friend, but rest assured, they are certainly not yours! People with focus and direction have no problem severing toxic relationships. They don't mind the criticism that is likely to ensue, because they are persuaded of who they are, and what they must do to succeed in life. To much of my surprise, I discovered that along with wealth comes criticism. You cannot have one without the other.

Athletes are always criticized by their fans. Their

every action is closely scrutinized and examined under the microscope of public opinion. Critics who don't have the guts to attempt what you actually achieve will always sit on the sideline yelling, "I wish I could get out there and show him what to do!" Your biggest critics will always know the least about what you do, but take it upon themselves to offer you the most input. Wealthy people are often criticized by those who are not, for no other purpose than because they are not. People who are not wealthy, usually hold the view that rich people are selfish, greedy pigs. OK, maybe I took this one too far. Wealth is not greed; greed is not wealth. Wealthy people do not object to losing friends; average people wail over them.

7. Wealthy people are usually people who are willing to give.

A strong financial sense and a strong moral sense go hand-in-hand. I believe that many investors and businesspeople are tired of the "greed is good" and or "profit at any cost" stereotype that most people hold regarding the investment or business industries. People want to feel good about making money. They like the fact that their money can do some good for charitable organizations, such as churches, the Feed the Children program, or the Red Cross. Sometimes the best way to approach heaven is by standing on your wallet. Wealthy people are the main contributors to charitable organizations. The average person gives less than 3 percent of his or her income to organizations that depend on freewill gifts for support. This may be part of the reason why average people remain average, while wealthy people continue to grow wealthier. The truly wealthy always share the wealth they have made.

8. Wealthy people are not indifferent towards having to work long hours.

Oftentimes, long hours are necessary especially, when one is initially starting a business, and this is one great deterrent for average people. People love their 9 to 5 hours too much to sacrifice their usual couch experience. Yet, they would love to experience the pleasures that wealthy people are privileged to enjoy without having to extract from their retirement investments to do so. Some things just take time, and it can prove to be time well spent. People of success are not clock watchers.

They would prefer to iron out the idea of a new proposal rather than go home to watch television. It's not that they are unwilling to spend time with their families, because in many cases these people spend quality time. Quantity is not as important as quality if all you're going to do is stay home and not communicate with your family. People of wealth can take long vacations with their families, visiting exotic islands, and taking Disney cruises to the Bahamas. The average person is stuck with borrowing money to go visit Aunt Sue and Uncle Joe in Florida. Instead of flying, they get a rental vehicle and spend much of their vacation time driving instead of vacationing. One way or another, if you don't spend time wisely and prepare for your future, you will eventually end up wasting time while engaging in unproductive activities.

The mark of a truly successful person is how much he or she is ultimately able to give back to the people that help them to succeed. No one person can ever say that they made it by their own merits. Money changes hands because people buy products. If no one buys into your dream, all you will have is a non-productive dream. You are the gardener who must plant his seed so that what is produced will ultimately feed nations. I've learned that the most individually successful people are actually the greatest servants of the common good. If successful wealthy people fall short in the area of giving, I can say with certainty that those people will lead miserable lives. If you only live for yourself, what good are you to others? Wealth is a blessing from above. The challenge lies in making money, but the greatest pleasure lies in sharing it!

Mastering The Fundamentals Of Success

"Your future success will rise or fall based on your willingness to submit to properly train."

~ **Mikel Brown**

Mastering The Fundamentals Of Success

I AM A FIRM BELIEVER THAT SUCCESS is not an accident. Unlike millions of Americans that play the lottery in hopes that they will one day buy the winning ticket, I believe that I am the winning ticket. Aristotle said, "Excellence is not an act, but a habit." Your future success will rise and fall based on your willingness to submit to proper training. Every winner in life has one common trait, they have learned to master the fundamentals of success. Michael Jordan, in my personal opinion, is arguably the greatest NBA player to ever play the game of basketball. It was often said by many of Michael's college and NBA teammates that during practice, he was usually the first one on the court and the last one to leave. Michael Jordan became great because he mastered the fundamentals of basketball. He was not just known for his ability to shoot jump shots, but free throws, slam dunks, lay ups, and he was an excellent defensive player. When the NBA players went to play in the 2004 Olympics, it was for certain that they would win the gold medal. In fact, many in the United States did not expect anything less than a gold medal. But as they played, it became painfully obvious that these guys had great jumping ability, excellent dribbling skills, and some of the best coaches in the NBA, but they had not learned to master the fundamentals. Everything in life has an origin or principle that governs success in a particular area. Meaning, you will not succeed if you have not learned the system or rules of engagement in your field of interest. Life itself has rules. Rules are the governing factors of everything on the planet. How well you learn and submit to those rules will determine the level of your success.

Mastering the fundamentals of success is imperative if you are going to move beyond your base level. It's similar to trying to pass a trigonometry or calculus test without understanding basic arithmetic. You know, as well as I do, that that will never happen. Your capacity to achieve in a certain area has already been predetermined by your willingness to listen to the kinds of words that will instruct you on how to succeed. Your readiness to prepare, and to be coached or mentored is evident of your passion and desire to succeed. You cannot escape this fundamental principle of success. When a business fails or a marriage is torn apart, or a test was flunked by a student, you better believe that those failures can be traced back to either refusing to listen to sound counsel, or the person chose to listen to the wrong voice. The success of your income has already been predetermined by your initial labor input. What you put into your training will be far greater in its return. The return is always greater than your initial investment, and the accolades will always exceed your training.

Secrets To Personal Success

*"You can never live beyond
your knowledge level."*

~ **Mikel Brown**

Secrets To Personal Success

SUCCESS IN ANYTHING DOES NOT come by accident. Your success must be deliberate. If you achieve any amount of success by chance or happenstance, you will lose it when you encounter your first challenge. The reason why the percentage of lottery winners going into bankruptcy is so high is because they never learned the lessons of how to handle money when they did not have much of it.

Your present capacity for where you are in life, may be at this time, only 6 inches in diameter (example). If you happen to get a lot of money through some state lottery, this is not an indication that your capacity has expanded. Your money may increase, but your capacity in character or life remains the same. Thus, as you continue to expose your newly acquired wealth to purchases, your income will rapidly diminish to your actual 6 inch in diameter sized capacity of money knowledge. You can never live beyond your knowledge level. Personal success comes from increasing your knowledge base, which causes your capacity to expand. How you handle money, people and business is indicative of what you have been taught concerning them. Let me give you a brief synopsis of how you can improve your personal success.

First, define what personal success is to you. There is no crime in thinking that "having more money" is how you define success. What is wrong is if money is the only element that will help you define success. Everyone needs money in our society, and you should not think that you are any different. Be honest with yourself. What secret motives prowl behind your desires? Would you like to show the naysayers that you did it without them or in spite of their lack of belief in your ability to succeed? If so, making more money will not only ruin you, but it will be used as a device to destroy other people. Genuinely change your motivation for wanting wealth. Convert it for the betterment of mankind and you will attract it from all sides.

Secondly, do not become inflexible as though you already have all the answers. Accomplishment only occurs when an extensive amount of training finally meets up with one moment of opportunity. People are turned off by know-it-alls. Usually, the one who feels they can do it without anyone's help will show that they cannot. My sales mentor once demonstrated one of the simplest ways of obtaining referrals. Everybody wants to help those that want their help and no one wants to help someone who acts as if they need none. Simply say to your clients after giving them your best service, "I need your help!" Briefly mention how they've helped you to help them and that you would like to help their friends and loved ones as well, and watch those referrals start pouring out. NO feeling is better than knowing that you have a hand in someone's success.

Thirdly, believe in yourself! You are your greatest asset and it's about time you start treating yourself like you are. One of the hardest thoughts to control is the one concerning you. All of what you can ever accomplish already exists in your being. You are the cause of where you are and you will be the one to propel yourself to where you're going.

If you would like to read more about developing your personal success, I highly recommend one of the greatest books I have ever written, "Building Wealth from the Ground Up". Invest in your image with the purchase of this book and buy one for your friends. They will thank you for caring for them.

Money Tips

"It's easy to save money by listening to sound advice."

~ **Mikel Brown**

Money Tips

I HAVE MORE INFORMATION THAT I believe will reestablish your focus, provide stamina to press forward towards your goals, and enable you to maneuver around and over obstacles designed to stop your progression. While you are dreaming of, I am dreaming up ways to help you fulfill your expectations. In this list of tips, I have something just for those who are partners and friends of mine. So, get ready and take out your three P's: pen, pencil, and paper. These items are necessary to chart your course, record and keep score. Remember, without a goal, how else are you going to know if you've won.

NO-LOAD STOCKS CAN BE BARGAINS

They are sold by companies to investors bypassing brokerage commissions. During the late 90s among the top firms offering no-load shares were Exxon, McDonald's, Mobil, and Procter & Gamble. Many smaller, riskier firms, also sell stocks directly to investors.

Advice: Buy directly if you want to accumulate the stock over a long period. No-load stocks are usually tied to dividend re-investments. Plan-dividends are used to pay for additional shares. Initial investments may only be $100 or $250.

DEBT REDUCTION

I strongly believe in being methodical, which in turn will help you in gauging or measuring how successful you really are in your endeavors to get out of debt. Do these eight things and you will succeed! Results may vary.

1. *Commit to change* by renovating your thinking concerning debt.
2. *Cash is king* - you cannot go into debt by paying cash for items.

3. *Track your spending,* even your lending.
4. *Attack your worst debt first,* which has more interest, and then go after the subsequent bills.
5. *Get a better rate* by asking your credit card company for a lower rate.
6. *Make a plan* and stick to it!
7. *Be aggressive and consistent* because diligence will pay off with less stress.
8. *Visualize yourself out of debt;* you cannot see, you cannot attempt. My new workout plan material is just what the doctor ordered. Find out more on how to get out of debt while building wealth.

HOW YOU CAN TURN $80 INTO OVER $1000 ANNUALLY

Millions of Americans literally give away thousands annually without their knowledge. I learned early in life the value of information. When I was only 18 years of age, a deacon in my church said to me, "Brother Brown, while you're young and single you should buy land while it is cheap." Today, that Deacon is in his eighties and very wealthy because he purchased land and sold it at a ridiculous 5000 to 20,000 percent profit. He was willing to give me all the information I needed in order to invest in land and real estate but I was young and ignorant and blew potentially millions of dollars by not valuing the information. Now, I am on a mission to prevent as many people as possible from making the same mistake. It's easy to save $1000 or more by listening to sound advice.

Let me give you a secret to keeping more of your money for investing, leisure, children's education funds, and family.

1. Banking – you can save $150-$250 a year. Most banks charge monthly check writing and or ATM fees that rapidly accumulate to as much as $300 a year on checking accounts.

Remedy: With the banks competition revving up their sales pitch to get more depositors, you can find a no fee checking account that requires a minimum balance. Don't be intimidated by the minimum balance. It can be worth shifting some money from one of your investments just so that you can maintain the minimum balance. Your loss can potentially be worse than you can imagine if you decide not to go with a checking account with a minimum balance, and no fees.

2. Credit Card Savings – is a mystery to most consumers. The majority of Americans are paying from three hundred dollars to over seven hundred and fifty dollars in finance charges and fees for a $2500 dollar balance.

Remedy: If you run a balance of $1000 or less on your credit card, a low interest rate will cut your debt in half. If you have made constant payments to your credit card company, you can call and ask them to give you a lower rate. Over 80 percent of credit card companies will honor your request. Stop using credit cards for cash advances because your company will assess a higher interest rate for cash. With just these two secrets, I saved over $1000. You will find more dollar saving tips in my books.

You can order my book entitled, "Building Wealth from the Ground Up", and gain more insightful ways to build and create wealth.

It's Good To Be A Winner

"Focus is the winner's advantage."

~ **Mikel Brown**

It's Good To Be A Winner

THERE IS AN OLD MAXIM THAT SAYS, "Good things come to those who wait." I personally differ with this age-old adage. Good things do not come to those who wait. Action is premiere for quintessential success. Excellence is rooted in control and stability. There are many would-be successful people who simply got tired of acting and seeing little results. So, they jumped on the bandwagon and waited. Focus is the winner's advantage. If you do not maintain attentiveness and give special attention to your goals, you will eventually find your aim in life void of a target.

A person genuinely needs objectives in order to

grow. Without these objectives, people will not have anything to reach for. Let's face it... Stuff happens! We cannot control everything in life because we cannot control other people. I can only work on me – turning my weaknesses into assets by simply delegating duties rather than remaining inactive. A person once said that the reason why they do not attempt much is because they do not want to make mistakes. Mistakes are not avoidable, nor are they final! They can work as gauges to help a person determine where their weaknesses may rest. Waiting does not denote inactivity. It is an active anticipation of occupying one's time until opportunity is presented, or until they can force it. However, action is needed if you are going to have any progress in your life.

Absolutely no one ever enjoys losing. It goes against human nature to be excited about losing. Whether you are playing sports, poker, applying for a new occupation or a new position on your job, losing at anything should not make you feel happy.

I am what you may call a sports enthusiast. I am competitive, but balanced. I am one who believes in competing against myself, although I may be playing against someone else. However, when I win against those opposing me, I know that it does something to their psyche. I am careful not to gloat over my win, but I enjoy watching the puzzled look on my opponent's faces. "Who is this man?" they often wonder. Winning is an art form. Once you learn the components of winning, you will find it easy to win in sports, business or in life and you will have discovered the power to influencing people. Without challenge, there can be no victory!

I have been busy dreaming and thinking of ways I can help you succeed in living your dream. I am of the old school of thought that says, "If I can assist others, in any small way, in living out God's determination for their lives, then my life will be worth that much more". Be the WINNER, you know you can BE!

First Principles of Wealth
The Groundwork of Increase

"Wealth is like a seed. A seed does not look like the forest it contains."

~ **Mikel Brown**

First Principles of Wealth
The Groundwork of Increase

WEALTH IS NOT FIRST MONEY—IT is principle. Money is the fruit, but principle is the root. The men and women who have shaped economies, altered industries, and forged legacies did not begin with overflowing bank accounts; they began with an overflowing belief that wealth is built, not wished.

Understanding the principle before the profit is critical to comprehending the why before the how. There are countless things to learn about wealth, yet the foundation of wealth is always established by principles—what we might also call laws. These laws are essential for mastering anything, especially wealth. Principles are eternal truths, set in place only by the Creator or manufacturer of a product. Is this essential to know? Yes, because without principles you may gain profit temporarily, but you will never sustain wealth permanently."

Wealth has always been about law before lifestyle. When you understand the laws of gravity, you can build planes. When you understand the laws of wealth, you can build empires. God, the Creator, is the Architect of wealth. "But thou shalt remember the LORD thy God: for it is he that giveth thee power to get wealth" (Deut. 8:18). Notice, He does not simply hand you money—He gives you power, capacity, ideas, resilience, and vision. The resource is divine; the responsibility is yours.

Below is a brief story of Wealth in the Hands of Visionaries:

John D. Rockefeller did not start as the titan of oil.

He was a bookkeeper earning mere dollars a week. But he mastered record-keeping, discipline, and tithing—principles that later allowed him to oversee one of the most powerful monopolies in history. He once said he began tithing on his first dollar, which later trained his soul to handle millions.

Henry Ford was not the first to build a car. But he grasped the principle of scaling. He asked: How can this be for the many, not the few? The assembly line was not just a mechanical invention—it was a wealth principle put into practice: multiplying capacity without multiplying cost.

Walt Disney was fired from a newspaper job for "lack of imagination." Yet he saw mice, castles, and stories where others saw nothing. The principle he mastered was imagination monetized. He turned dreams into destinations, and vision into revenue.

Warren Buffett began by buying his first stock at age 11. He did not wait for a million to practice—he practiced with three shares. His principle: start small, but start with mastery. He built a fortress by first stacking pebbles.

Larry Ellison, orphaned and raised in humble circumstances, created Oracle by seeing the future of databases. He didn't begin with wealth; he began with a problem he believed he could solve better than anyone else. His principle: opportunity hides in plain sight for the one willing to believe.

I want you to grasp the humble beginnings of these men so that you can believe for yourself that humility may not look lofty, but it is the strongest launchpad to reach greatness. From humility, you see clearer, dream bigger, and rise higher. Every story screams the same truth: wealth is always birthed in principle before it is ever seen in profit.

God's Wealth Blueprint is a God Thang!

Wealth is God's idea. He laid gold in the Garden before Adam sinned (Gen. 2:12). He gave Joseph strategy to feed nations in famine. He gave Solomon wisdom that drew rulers bearing treasures. The principle is divine partnership—God gives the seed, but man must sow it.

Here is the critical key: You don't have to have wealth to begin living by the principles of wealth. You need only belief and discipline. Wealth begins in your mindset.

- Principle One: Stewardship. If you cannot manage a paycheck, you cannot manage a fortune. Jesus said, "He that is faithful in that which is least is faithful also in much" (Luke 16:10).

- Principle Two: Multiplication. Wealth is not in what you consume, but in what you multiply. The talents in Matthew 25 reveal that the one who multiplied was trusted with cities..

- Principle Two: Multiplication. Wealth is not in what you consume, but in what you multiply. The talents in Matthew 25 reveal that the one who multiplied was trusted with cities.

- Principle Three: Vision. Wealth gravitates to the one who sees further. Without vision, money becomes waste. With vision, money becomes multiplication.

- Principle Four: Generosity. Rockefeller, Carnegie, and others understood giving as power. When money flows through you, more will flow to you. "The liberal soul shall be made fat" (Prov. 11:25).

Wealth is like a seed. A seed does not look like the forest it contains. It is small, unimpressive, and easily overlooked. But in the right soil, watered with belief, disciplined with stewardship, and protected by vision, it grows into a forest that feeds generations. You don't need the forest in your hand—you need the seed in your spirit.

My Personal Proof – Dr. Mikel Brown

When I began my journey, I did not begin with millions. I began with principles. I started restaurants, publishing, an advertising agency, schools, and now even a credit union—each venture rooted in stewardship, multiplication, vision, and generosity. I was not born into wealth, but I was born into potential. By applying kingdom principles, I learned to turn little into much.

I remember the early days—limited capital, but unlimited conviction. I knew if I could manage the resources in my hand, God would multiply what was beyond my reach. Those principles carried me from ideas on paper to buildings on land, from private prayers to public enterprises.

- "The blessing of the LORD, it maketh rich, and he addeth no sorrow with it" (Prov. 10:22).

- "I wisdom dwell with prudence, and find out knowledge of witty inventions" (Prov. 8:12)

- "Cast thy bread upon the waters: for thou shalt find it after many days" (Eccl. 11:1).

These are wealth principles disguised as scriptures: blessing, wisdom, innovation, and sowing. They are divine invitations to walk in wealth without guilt.

Yes, if it sounds like I'm working up a fire in you to believe, it is because I am. My aim is to be explosive with encouragement which is needed to propel you into wealth. The doors of wealth are not locked—they are simply hidden from the untrained eye. When you learn the first principles,

Wealth Requires Belief:

The greatest poverty is not lack of money—it is lack of belief. The wealthy are those who believe first, build second, and bank last. You don't need Wall Street to validate you. You don't need millions to get started. You need conviction that wealth is a discipline, not an accident.

> "Wealth is not found in the coins you count, but in the convictions you keep."
> —Dr. Mikel Brown

A paycheck is like a stream; wealth is like a reservoir. If you only drink, you'll stay thirsty. If you dam and direct the flow, you'll create rivers for generations.

A Biblical Anchor for Wealth Builders

The Bible is not silent on wealth, and here are a few scriptures to prove it:

you begin to see opportunities everywhere: in your paycheck, in your community, in your imagination.

- A paycheck is not your prison; it is your practice ground.

- A small business is not your limitation; it is your laboratory.

- A single idea is not your end; it is your entry point.

"It doesn't take a fortune to birth one—it takes foresight, faith, and follow-through."
—Dr. Mikel Brown

Wealth is not reserved for the elite. You don't have to be a millionaire or billionaire to be wealthy. Wealth is a mindset, a stewardship, and a divine partnership. If you can manage your paycheck, you can manage your wealth. If you can govern your little, you can be trusted with much.

The men who built empires were not given the keys—they forged them through principle. And the same God who gave them seed, strategy, and success has placed the same potential in you.

So rise. Believe. Apply. Practice the principles. For the door to your future does not open with money in hand—it opens with wealth in mind.

About The Author

DR. MIKEL BROWN is an author, businessperson, restaurateur, and religious leader who resides in El Paso, Texas. He is a Licensed Professional Counselor with more than 40 years of experience. He has helped many people achieve success in business, marriage, personal development and peak performance.

Dr. Brown has helped people from rocky marriages to rocketing careers. His private client protégés list range from active and retired professional sports personalities to more than a hundred small business owners. He has over 14 books published, such as *When Lambs Turns Into Lions, Dream Big Start Small, Turn on Your Life, Unexpected Treasures, How to Fix Your Marriage without Using a Hammer,* and *Building Wealth from the Ground Up.*

THE POCKET MOTIVATOR BOOK SERIES

DR. MIKEL A. BROWN

Now You Can Take The Wisdom of Dr. Brown With You Wherever You Go!

GET YOUR COPIES
TODAY!

www.MikelBrown.com

www.ingramcontent.com/pod-product-compliance
Lightning Source LLC
Chambersburg PA
CBHW061805070526
44586CB00023B/2719